THAT'S ALL! ELLEN'LL BE GIVING A DISPLAY OF PISTOL-SHOOTING AT THE *RED OX SALOON* TONIGHT!

PISTOLS? RIFLES? WHAT DOES SHE DO FOR AN *ENCORE?*

PUNCH COWS? WRESTLE BULLS?

THAT'S ENOUGH OF THAT, BRET...

MISS ELLEN, MY SO-CALLED PARTNER IN THE RED OX, *BRET MAVERICK*...

HOWDY...DO *ALL* THE GIRLS SHOOT LIKE THAT WHERE YOU COME FROM?

IN TROY, NEW YORK? NO! I THINK I'M THE ONLY ONE...

ELLEN... OF *TROY?!*

MY FATHER, MANUEL FORTUNE...

SIR...

WELL, EXCUSE US... WE'VE GOT TO GET BACK TO THE RED OX...DELIGHTFUL TO HAVE YOU VISIT OUR TOWN, MISS ELLEN...

OTHER VISITORS, HOWEVER, ARE BY NO MEANS SO PLEASANT...

HOWDY, GUTHRIE... HEAR YOU'RE NOT SHERIFF ANY MORE...

DON'T GIVE ME NO TROUBLE, PARRISH...

Gambling Out West

Gambling was the most popular means of recreation in the Wild West. In every cattle town, mining camp, military fort, and isolated log cabin, wherever a bunch of cowboys or Westerners gathered to relax you could bet your boots that a game of cards would soon be in progress.

Booming cowtowns in Kansas, gold mining camps in California, Colorado and Montana, and railroad construction camps attracted the professional gamblers – slick, skilful, ice-cool characters experienced in parting "suckers" from their money. There were many gentlemen cardsharps like Ben Maverick, some were honourable players, others were dishonest and arguments and gunfights over cheating were numerous.

Most Westerners were armed in those tough times and the professional gambler was no exception. He usually kept a small but deadly pocket pistol out of sight, handy for any trouble that might explode over the gaming table. The cardsharp, be he honest or crooked, had to rely on his quick wits and tricks of the trade to survive in the jungle conditions of the Wild West. Accused by an angry loser of cheating, the cardsharp could either talk his way out of trouble – or shoot his way out.

Gambler "Diamond Dick" Danvers found himself in a desperate situation one evening in Dodge City, Kansas, in 1870, having won a pile of money from a notorious badman, Eli Monk. "Maybe I can't prove it, but I'm sure you cheated me," snarled Monk, pulling out his Colt revolver. "Nobody fools me and lives to laugh about it." Danvers stared calmly into the barrel of the six-shooter and appealed to the gunman. "I am unarmed. If you shoot me it will be murder, not self defence, as these gentlemen will witness."

Monk's eyes flashed to the others in the saloon. All were

Above: *A poker game at Dodge City where Governor Carney lost a great deal.* Right: *Eli Monk threatens to mutilate gambler Dick Danvas for cheating.*

silent, closely watching the tense situation. Monk was not liked and witnesses would readily speak against him. "You're right, card shark," said the badman with a wicked grin. "I won't shoot you. I got a better idea. I'm gonna cut off your cheating fingers so you won't play cards again."

Monk holstered his gun and drew a big bowie knife. "Gimme your hand!" he demanded of Danvers. The gambler extended his diamond-bedecked right hand across the table. Next instant the outstretched hand was a fist, filled with a little derringer pocket pistol, the discharge of which shattered the silence. Eli Monk staggered back and fell dead, an expression of surprise fixed on his face.

Dick Danvers departed the saloon as swiftly as the hidden pistol had sprung into his hand. The derringer had been concealed up his sleeve, secured to a wrist strap by a small spring. Pressure on the spring had delivered the gun straight into his hand for firing. The same kind of device was also employed to deliver crooked cards to the hand.

Some professional gamblers accused, or proved guilty on the spot of cheating were either lynched by an angry mob or shot dead by the so-called "mark" or "sucker." An old grave at Boot Hill, Dodge City, carried the simple epitaph: "Here Lies Red Ike. He Held Five Aces." When gambler Pat Hogan was shot dead an ace of hearts was found in his pocket, on which he had written:

"Life is only a game of poker,
played well or ill
Some hold four aces; some
draw and fill
Some make a bluff and oft
get there
While others ante and never
hold a pair."

One card cheat, finding himself under growing suspicion from the other players, ordered up a sandwich, slipped his crooked cards between the slices of bread and began to eat it. The others knew what was happening and let him get on with his thoroughly unpleasant meal. From that day on he was dubbed "Eat 'Em Up Jake."

Saloons and casinos provided various types of gambling - cards, dice, roulette, and keno, the latter being a kind of bingo. Card games, however, were the most popular and these included seven-up, black jack, monte, faro, and poker. Most of these games of chance were of foreign origin and entered the United States through New Orleans, the fountain head of gambling in America.

Elegant New Orleans, and her splendid steamboats that plied the Mississippi River, gave rise to the prototype professional gambler, soft-spoken and fashionably dressed, a gentleman of the gaming table. During the 1850s some 2,000 professional gamblers worked the steamboats on the Mississippi. With gambling the consuming passion of his gentlemen passengers, the steamboat captain tolerated and even encouraged the cardsharps. Games would go on for hours and marathon affairs for days. Stakes were often high – 10,000 or 25,000 dollars on a single hand. When cash ran out a plantation owner might put up his entire estate on the turn of a card.

From New Orleans the gamblers moved westward as the great wilderness was opened to settlement. When new towns were founded on gold strikes

the card sharks soon arrived to part gullible prospectors from their newly-acquired wealth. In his book *Vigilante Days and Ways,* N. P. Langford describes the gold town Virginia City, Nevada, in the 1860s:

"Gold was abundant and every possible device was employed by the gamblers, the traders, the vile men and women that had come with the miners, to obtain it. Nearly every third cabin in the town was a saloon where vile whiskey was peddled for fifty cents a drink in gold dust. Many of these places were filled with gambling tables and gamblers, and the miner who was bold enough to enter one of them with his day's earnings in his pocket, seldom left until thoroughly fleeced."

As the railroads pushed West the armies of well-paid construction workers set up mobile base towns, here today, gone tomorrow, which attracted saloon keepers and professional gamblers. These roaring, temporary tent-towns were known as "Hell on Wheels" because of the many fights and murders triggered by drink and gambling. More than once the railroad owners had to call in the army to clear out the troublemakers.

Abilene, Kansas, was the first of the cowtowns, the end of trail railheads from where the cattle, driven up by Texas cowboys, were transported east by train. Abilene was divided by the railroad into two sections. The north side was the respectable section with churches, banks and businesses. The south side – called "Little Texas" – was the wild part of town where the saloons, dance halls and gambling casinos catered for the rowdy, free-spending Texas cowboys who had been paid off after their long trail drive.

Cowboys were enthusiastic poker players. The game probably originated in Persia and later found its way to France and Germany where it was, known, respectively, as *poque* and *pochen,* from which came the English corruption of "poker." Cowboy phrases relating to the game have become part of the English language, such as "passing the buck," "ace in the hole," "ace high," "cold deck," "showdown" and "square deal." Cowboys also bet on horse races between their best riders, and on who could keep in the saddle of a bucking mustang, the latter sport being the origin of the

A faro game in Morenci, Arizona Territory, in the 1880s.

rodeo. They would also wager as to which of two fighting bulls would put the other to flight.

When Frank Leslie made his famous tour of the Wild West in 1877 he reported in his newspaper that gambling in the frontier town of Cheyenne, Wyoming, "far from being merely an amusement or recreation, rises to the dignity of a legitimate occupation — the persuit of nine-tenths of the population, both permanent and transient. There are twenty gambling saloons in this little town, the proprietors of which pay yearly licenses of 600 dollars for each table."

Gambling was a passion in every level of society. In 1877 the Dodge City *Times* reported a notable poker game in which the ex-governor of the State, Thomas Carney, came to the famous Kansas cattle town to buy "hides and bones for a St. Louis firm." It became clear from later developments that Carney's real business in Dodge City was to entice some prominent local citizens into a heavy

game of draw poker, at which he considered himself a sharp hand. But he came a cropper when he sat down with three businessmen, including Colonel Norton.

"At last the governor held what he supposed to be an invincible hand," ran the report in the *Times*. "It consisted of four kings and the cuter, or 'Imperial trump,' which the governor very reasonably supposed to be the ace of spades . . . Governor Carney's eyes glistened with joy as he saw the pile of treasure which would soon be his own loom up before his vision, and he hastened to "see" the colonel and add the remainder of his funds, his elegant gold watch and chain. Norton was still with the game and the governor finally stripped himself of all remaining valuables, when it became necessary for him to show his hand.

"A breathless silence pervaded the room as governor Carney spread his four kings on the table with his left hand and

encircled the glittering heap of gold, silver, greenbacks, and precious stones with his right arm, preparatory to raking in the spoils. But at that moment a sight met the governor's gaze which caused his eyes to dilate with terror . . . Right in front of Colonel Norton were spread four genuine and perfectly formed aces . . . Slowly and reluctantly the governor uncoiled his arm from around the sparkling treasure."

Governor Carney left Dodge on the next east-bound train, minus his gold watch and personal jewellery, "bowed down with overwhelming grief," as the *Times* gleefully commented. "Governor Carney is not buying bones and hides in this city any more."

A number of celebrated lawmen and gunfighters were noted gamblers, such as Wyatt Earp, Wild Bill Hickok, Doc Holliday and Luke Short. We shall meet these characters and follow their fortunes in Part Two, called GAMBLERS AND GUNMEN.

THE GARNER FILES

Name:	James Garner.
Real name:	James Bumgarner.
Profession:	Actor; producer; businessman.
Previous jobs:	Chauffeur (at 14!), clothes salesman, grocery store assistant, tree-cutter for telephone company, waiter, oil-well worker, lifeguard, janitor, construction worker, dish-washer, truck driver, window decorator, golfball retriever, poolroom manager, pool hustler, insurance salesman, petrol station attendant, swimwear model, merchant marine, national guardsman and soldier . . .
Born:	April 7, 1928.
Birthplace:	Norman, Oklahoma.
Parents:	Mildred and Weldon Bumgarner (Mildred died when Jim was five; his father later married Wilma).
Father's profession:	Upholsterer and carpet-layer.
Family:	Two elder brothers: Charles, a schoolteacher; and Jack, once a baseball player for the Pittsburgh Pirates, now a golf professional — and part-time actor in Jim's TV shows.

Wife:	Lois Clarke; they married in 1956.
Children:	Two daughters. Kimberly, born August 25, 1948 to Mrs. Garner's previous marriage; and Greta Scott, born January 4, 1958, known as Gigi, she recently cut her first disc in London.
Resident:	Beverly Hills.
Height:	6 ft. 3 ins.
Weight:	190 lbs.
Education:	Grade school in Norman, his home town; Hollywood High School; Norman High School; Frank Williams Trade School, 'where I majored in first-aid and that's no joke'; University of Oklahoma at 24, after Korean war service, studying business administration. He dropped out after one term — having learned enough judging by his later business success.
Military service:	Merchant Marine at 16, for one year, working on a tug-boat out of New Orleans; Oklahoma State National Guard at 17; then 14 months in the Korean war as an infantryman with the Fifth Regimental Combat Team of the 24th Division.
Discoverer:	Stage producer Paul Gregory.
Acting debut:	Non-speaking role as one of the six judges in *The Cain Mutiny Court Martial* with Henry Fonda on Broadway, 1954. He later understudied one of the roles and played one of the leading parts in a post-Broadway tour of the play.
TV debut:	As a Cavalry lieutenant in the premier episode of Clint Walker's tele-Western series, *Cheyenne,* 1955. Result: a Warner Brothers' contract . . . and soon enough his own Western series. (And Jim's Maverick was to outdistance Walker's by 138 shows to 106).
Film debut:	*Toward The Unknown* with the late William Holden and Lloyd Nolan, 1956. This seven-minute debut was immediately followed by playing a GI in *The Girl He Left Behind.* In 1957, Jim went West for *Shoot out At Medicine Bend.* In the same year he made *Sayonara.*
First TV series:	*Maverick* — as gambler Bret Maverick, brother of the rapidly introduced Jack Kelly' Bart, cousin to Roger Moore's Beau (joining the series when Jim Garner quit). Starting in 1957, the series ran until 1962; Jim also appeared in it, every so often as the brothers' father — Pappy Beauregard Maverick!
First film break:	Taking over the lead in *The Young Invaders* war-movie (US title: *Darby's Rangers),* 1958.
Later early films:	1959 Gordon Douglas' *Up Periscope.* 1960 *Cash McCall.* 1962 William Wyler's *The Loudest Whisper* (US: *The Children's Hour).* Michael Gordon's MGM comedy, *Boy's Night Out* had Jim and Tony Randall chasing after Kim Novak.
Busiest film year:	1963 John Sturges' *The Great Escape,* prisoner-of-war epic with Steve McQueen, Charles Bronson, James Coburn and

James Garner as he appeared in the original Maverick *series way back in 1957.*

Richard Attenborough. Norman Jewison's *The Thrill Of It All.* Arthur Hiller's *Separate Beds* (US: *The Wheeler Dealers*). Michael Gordon's *Move Over Darling* which became the Royal Film Performance choice for 1964 in London . . . which was handy as that's where Jim was due to shoot . . .

'My best film':	1964	Arthur Hiller's *The Americanisation of Emily.*
Later films:	1965	George Seaton's *36 Hours,* Norman Jewison's *The Art of Love.*
Another hectic year:	1966	*A Man Could Get Killed* with Melina Mercouri. Delbert Mann's *Woman Without A Face* (US: *Mister Buddwing*). Amnesia drama from the Evan Hunter novel.
Another favourite film:	1966	John Frankenheimer's *Grand Prix* with Jim in his element — in the driver's seat doing most of his own motor-racing on all the Euro grand prix circuits.

Still more films:	1967	John Sturges' *Hour of the Gun* a kind of sequel to Sturges' *Gunfight at the O.K. Coral.*
	1968	*How Sweet It Is* with Debbie Reynolds. Delbert Mann's *The Pink Jungle,* made by Garner's company.
	1969	*Marlowe* put Garner back on top. He was only the fifth actor to play Raymond Chandler's laconic private eye hero. Director Paul Bogart's film modernised the character...but it worked. Based on the Chandler novel, *The Little Sister. Support Your Local Sheriff* was a better Garner production than *Jungle,* sending up his *Maverick* heroics.
Into his third decade:	1970	*A Man Called Sledge,* an Italian spaghetti Western.
	1971	*Support Your Local Gunfighter,* the inevitable sequel to the terrific William Bowers' *Sheriff* script. Paul Bogart's *Skin Game,* hilarious Western comedy, with Garner as a con-man.
Favourite TV series:	1971	*Nichols,* produced by Jim's Cherokee company, ran one season (26 shows) only.
Back to movies:	1972	James Goldstone's *They Only Kill Their Masters,* a small-town murder mystery with Jim as a (wry, of course) police chief.
	1973	Garner goes Disney for Bernard McEveety's *One Little Indian.* Anti-heroic as ever, Jim was a US Cavalry deserter (he'd been sentenced to hang for trying to save Indian women and children in battle) who befriends a white boy reared as an Indian, and trying to return to his tribe.
	1974	Garner stays Disney for a family movie encore: Vincent McEveety's *The Castaway Cowboy.* This time, Jim swopped camels for cattle — and the first cattle ranch in Hawaii in the 1880s.
First TV Movie:	1974	Or March 27, to be precise about the day Jim first opened *The Rockford Files* — in the pilot film for a possible series, made by his company and Universal. Richard T. Heffron directed and it was scripted and produced by Stephen J. Cannell, but the tele-Jim is very much Garner's creation.
Third TV series:	1974 1980	The pilot was a winner and *The Rockford Files* became an immediate hit series from September 13, 1974. Just as *Maverick* had been the last of the Westerns, *Rockford* survived all the *Kojaks, Columbos* and *Barettas* as the last of the good cop-shows.
Second TV Movie:	1978	*The New Maverick.* So many critics had begun comparing *Rockford* to *Maverick,* Jim's Cherokee company decided to bring the series back — starring a member of the family. Charles Frank was Ben Maverick, son of Brett and Bart's British cousin, Beau. Garner and Jack Kelly guest-starred as the brothers, unseen since 1962. Jim also appeared in the opening episode of the *Young Maverick* short-lived series (1979-80), starring Charles Frank and his actress wife, Susan Blanchard.
Last movies:	1979	Robert Altman's *Health.*
	1981	Edward Bianchi's *The Fan* co-starring for the second

*1970 and Garner's still in the
saddle, this time in the
spaghetti western, A Man
Called Sledge.*

consecutive time, Lauren Bacall.
Blake Edwards' *Victor, Victoria.*

One that got away: 1981 was also the year Jim Garner went to Canada in order
to make the *Pure Escape* film. All started well enough but
sadly, the film remains unfinished due to Canadian finance
difficulties. Little wonder, therefore, that Jim went straight
back to...

Third TV movie: 1981   *Bret Maverick*...rides again! A new Garner company,
Comanche, but an old role — his best, most classically pure
Garner. The best of the Maverick clan, twenty years after
we left him out West...now set up in Sweetwater, Arizona,
running the Red Ox Saloon. Stuart Margolin directed the
two-hour pilot show, which introduced most of the
characters delighting us in...

Fouth TV series: 1981   *Bret Maverick* — the series that puts James Garner where
he should be again. At the top!

Bret Maverick leaned back against the bar and let his gaze wander round the Red Ox Saloon with mixed feelings. On the one hand, he was disappointed at the fewer than average number of customers that afternoon; on the other, he was glad to have it quiet and peaceful while Tom Guthrie was out of town for a couple of days. Being left in charge was all very well so long as there was no trouble brewing up...but he was looking forward to Guthrie's return on the following morning.

Maybe, Bret thought, he would have felt more settled if he could have organised a reasonable game of poker, but unfortunately all the locals knew him too well to throw their money away, and the only strangers in the saloon were a couple of mean looking cowboys who seemed intent on propping up the bar and drinking until the bar had to prop them up. Bret could tell they were well on the way from their tone of voice, and shrugged wearily, hoping he wouldn't have to throw them out. That sort of thing could ruin a man's day...

If it wasn't going to be ruined sooner. From the doorway, he could hear raised voices, and turned to see Joe, the new bar-hand, arguing with a blond-haired youth who was trying to make his way inside. The cause of the trouble was obvious: the newcomer had a Colt 45 strapped low on his thigh, and didn't seem at all inclined to part with it. Shaking himself, Bret straightened up and headed toward the door.

"No way..." the youth was saying coldly. "Where I go, the gun goes..."

"Look, I'm sorry, fella..." began Joe, trying to explain again. Bret threw his shoulders back, trying to look authoritative, and decided to make his presence felt.

"Having trouble, Joe?" he asked calmly, trying not to look at the fair-haired youth. There was a mean, cold cast to the kid's face which Bret didn't like at all.

"It's the gun, Mister Maverick..." Joe said tiredly, gesturing toward the newcomer, and Bret turned to face him for the first time.

"House rule, son..." Bret began, then,

OUT OF THE PAST

looking at the youth's face, instantly realised he'd made a mistake. One thing you never call a mean young man with a gun and an itchy trigger-finger is 'son'. Bret took a deep breath and began again.

"We get some tough hombres in the Red Ox," he said. "Now, we don't mind...we'll take the meanest...but we don't like trouble. You see, I've got a nervous barman..." Bret glanced round over his shoulder and pointed toward Jack, who had sidled up to the near end of the bar and was now pointing a large double-barrelled shot-gun in their direction.

"And Jack just *hates* blowing the heads off people, don't you, Jack?" Jack nodded, his aim never wandering from the youth. "Now, are you coming in, or staying out in the street?"

The young gunslinger looked sullenly from Jack to Bret, back to Jack again, and then smiled ruefully, pulling the Colt from his holster and handing it over.

"Now I like a man with sense..." smiled Bret, clapping the kid on the shoulder and walking toward the bar with him. "And just to show that

the management of the Red Ox appreciates co-operative customers, the first drink's on the house. What'll you have?"

"A beer..." was the reply as they approached the bar. Maverick noticed the two cowboys looking in their direction, and there was resentment in their gaze. But hell, he couldn't give everyone in the place free drinks. Bret led the newcomer a couple of yards further down the bar and called for a beer.

"What's your name?" Bret asked, as the beer slid toward them along the bar-top.

"Brody," came the reply, as the kid picked up the glass and gulped thirstily. "Sam Brody."

"Just passing through?" enquired Bret.

"Maybe...maybe not..." said Brody, putting down the half drunk glass of beer and looking at Bret suspiciously. Then, glancing down at the beer again and deciding that he owed it to Bret to be civil, reached into his pocket and pulled out a crumpled old piece of paper, which he began to smooth out on the bar. "I'm looking for this fella here," he explained. "Heard tell he was someplace in Sweetwater..."

Bret looked down at the Wanted poster and pretended to study the hand-drawn portrait, though he knew well enough whose likeness it was. *'Tom Blaylock'* the wording read. *'Wanted for murder. Reward: Five thousand Dollars. Dead or Alive'*. And Tom Blaylock, Bret knew, was none other than his partner in the Red Ox Saloon, Tom Guthrie.

"Haven't seen him..." Bret said, trying to keep the poster out of everyone else's sight. The murder charge was twelve years old, and Tom Guthrie had led a blameless life ever since, even being sheriff of Sweetwater for most of that time, but Bret figured it was inevitable that someone would track him down eventually. But he hadn't expected anyone as young as Brody, who couldn't have been more than about five years old when the poster was first printed.

"I remember hearing about the guy, though," continued Bret. "Mean as a one-legged coyote! And pretty fast with a gun...one of the fastest, as I recall..."

Maybe I can frighten him off before Tom gets back tomorrow, Bret thought to himself. It wasn't going to work though.

"Can't scare me, fella!" Brody said with a thin smile, unconsciously reaching toward his holster, then pausing as he remembered it was empty. "I'm good, and I know it! The best! Blaylock's just going to be the *first*...then I'm gonna build up a real reputation!"

"Always someone faster..." shrugged Bret, trying to bring that particular line of conversation to a halt as he saw the two drunks staring in their direction.

"I'll be at the hotel," said Brody, draining his glass and looking around at the saloon's customers before picking up the poster and putting it back in his pocket. "You see this Blaylock fella, you let me know. I'll make it worth your while..."

Brody turned to go, only to walk straight into the nearest of the two drunks. Words of apology started from his lips, then stopped. He began to push past the drunk toward the door.

"Where d'ya think you're going, sonny-boy?" spat the drunk, and started to swing a wildly off-target punch. Bret groaned inwardly and turned toward Jack behind the bar, but the shot-gun was already up and in his hands.

"Outside!" commanded Bret, though he was sure the shot-gun provided a much more telling argument. Brody and the drunks headed toward the door, picked up their guns, and stepped out on to the sidewalk.

Bret turned toward Jack and started to call for a drink, then stopped as he heard the argument continuing outside, and getting angrier by the second. He started across the saloon, paused at the bat-wing doors, and looked out.

Brody and one of the drunks had already stepped out into the street and were facing off, hands hovering near their gunbelts. Bret stepped out onto the sidewalk, trying to think of something he could say that would stop the inevitable gun-fight, but is was already too late.

The drunk was lamentably slow, it was true, but before his gun had even cleared leather, Brody had put a bullet through his arm. The kid was fast, there was no doubt.

As the suddenly sobered cowboy clutched his arm and staggered off looking for the doctor, Brody coolly re-holstered his gun and glanced round toward Bret, as if looking for praise.

"Always someone faster..." Bret told him again, and then turned back into the Red Ox.

Leaving the Lazy Ace first thing the following morning, Bret rode swiftly into town, visited the local gunsmith, moved hurriedly past the hotel and made sure there was no sign of Brody on the street yet, and then rode away again. A couple of miles up the trail to Grandon Rapids he stopped, tied Lo-Ball to a tree, and settled down to wait, cleaning and checking an old revolver he'd brought with him from the ranch. This was the road that Tom Guthrie would have to take on his return, and he'd find Bret waiting for him.

An hour passed and the sun rose higher in the sky before Bret saw a lone horseman riding toward him slowly. Mounting up, Bret rode toward him, waving an arm in friendly greeting.

"Funny way you've got of looking after our saloon," growled Tom Guthrie as Bret rode up to meet him, but the latter was in no mood to argue the point.

"We've got trouble, Tom," Bret explained. "Or more to the point, you've got trouble…" And Bret swiftly explained all he knew about Sam Brody.

"You could always ride back to Grandon Rapids for a few days," suggested Bret. "Brody might figure he's wasting his time if there's no sign of you and move on…"

"He might," replied Tom thoughtfully. "Or he might just stick around for weeks. No, that's no good, Bret. I knew something like this was bound to happen one day, and now it has…well, I guess I've just got to face up to it…"

"Maybe," said Bret, "but this kid's fast. Fast as anyone I've seen. And you can't be anywhere near as good as you used to be, Tom. A dead partner's not going to be much help running the Red Ox…!"

Guthrie continued to walk his horse toward Sweetwater, lost in thought.

"How about I sneak up and shoot Brody in the back?" suggested Bret, but Guthrie shook his head, as expected. "Well, we could knock him over the head, nail him into a crate and stick him on a train to someplace…"

"He'd only be back…" Guthrie told him.

Tom Guthrie's answers had been pretty much as Bret expected. He shrugged and started to explain his final plan. "Listen, I've been thinking about this overnight. Way I see it, the only way we can handle this is to use an old poker-player's trick. We bluff. It's kind of dangerous…for *both* of us…which is why I didn't mention it before, and the whole thing rests on my judgement of Brody's character, which is why *you* won't like it, but it goes something like this…"

After ten minutes of talk and explanation, Bret kicked Lo-Ball into a gallop and headed back to Sweetwater, leaving Guthrie to follow at a walking pace. He circuited the town and came to the Red Ox by the back way, tied up his horse and headed within. Walking through the saloon to the

front door, he looked out across Main Street.

Sam Brody had just come out of the hotel, and was now settling himself on a tilted back chair on the sidewalk, cleaning his gun and watching the street. Fortunately it was still early, and there weren't too many people around.

Bret took a deep breath, checked his revolver and gun belt, nerved himself for what he was about to do, and stepped out onto the street. Crossing over toward the hotel, he leaned on the hitching rail and greeted Brody.

"You heard anything of Blaylock yet?" asked Brody.

"No...and maybe it's a good job, too...said Bret, glancing up the street. Tom Guthrie ought to be riding into town any moment now. "You thought any more about what I said yesterday? About there always being someone faster than you?"

"A little, maybe..." Brody admitted, thrusting his gun into his holster. "But it goes with the job, doesn't it! I was brung up by sheep-herders, Mister Maverick, and believe me, there ain't no more miserable existence than that! What kind of life am I gonna have as a farm-boy? So it's Blaylock or me...what do I care?"

Bret glanced up the street again, and saw Guthrie approaching at last. There was no more time to argue the point with Brody now. "Think about it," he said, turning away.

Sam Brody watched Maverick walk off up the street, pondering. Maybe he was just a gambler, and his Ma had always told him that sort were the scum of the earth, but there was a guy who'd made something of himself. His own saloon, friends...and Maverick was the first person he'd met since he left the farm who'd treated him like a grown man. He watched as Maverick walked up to the approaching horseman and stopped, about thirty yards away.

The newcomer dismounted, tied his horse to the rail, and started talking to Maverick. Some sort of argument seemed to break out between them, but in spite of the silence of the deserted street, Brody couldn't hear what it was about. But the voices grew louder, and then he heard one word of Maverick's...

"Blaylock".

Instantly, Brody was on his feet, hand at his belt. But before he could move, Maverick and the stranger had stepped apart, and Maverick was drawing back his jacket, clearing his holster. Brody's surprise turned to horror as he saw Maverick go for the gun, and then two shots rang out.

Brody's eyes had been on Maverick, so he didn't see the other man draw...but it must have been fast. For the gambler was falling forward on his face, and as he did so, Blaylock fired another four shots at him, emptying the revolver. While Brody stared in shock, Blaylock started across the street toward the Red Ox, already starting to reload his gun.

"Blaylock!" called Brody, stepping out onto the street, hand near his gun-butt, but noticing a nervous tremble run up his arm as he did so. "There's always someone faster..." Those had been Maverick's words. Virtually his last words. Brody's eyes flickered toward the body laying face down in the street.

"What?" growled Tom Guthrie, re-holstering his gun, fully loaded. Brody stared at him, tried to speak, found he couldn't. He tried to look into his opponent's eyes, but found a piercing stare that he couldn't match.

"Well?" barked Guthrie.

"Uh, nothing..." said Brody weakly, and turned hurriedly away, heading back to the hotel. Behind him, Jack and Joe ran out of the Red Ox and carried Maverick inside.

"Guess it worked then..." said Bret, sighing with relief, as soon as he was safely out of sight inside the saloon. "Sure glad I picked up those blank cartridges from the store this morning!"

Guthrie gave him an unaccustomed grin as Bret started brushing the dust from his clothes. "I figure that if I worked on him a little first, and then let him see you shoot me 'dead', his nerve would crack. Seems a shame that Brody's gonna head back to the farm now, but..."

"Oh, I don't know," said Tom, looking out the window and seeing Brody mounting his horse and galloping out of town at high speed. "He seems in an awful hurry to get back there!"

Cowboy trail boss in Montana, 1887.

Chief Wasakie, famous chief of the Shoshoni tribe, born about 1804 and died in 1900.

Cowboys in Dodge City, Kansas, pose for the photographer in the 1880s.

HOW IT ALL BEGAN.....

It sure takes some believing, but it is close on twenty-five years — yes, a quarter of a century — since James Garner first delighted the world with his wry, laconic, anti-heroic gamblin' man called Bret Maverick. Shooting began on August 20, 1957.

He had little idea the show would make him a star. But at least he started out dressed as a star. Like Errol Flynn, in fact. Garner's Maverick wore Flynn's jacket and waist-coat from a 1950 horse-opera Flynn had made with his then wife, Patrice Wymore. The film had been called *Rocky Mountain*...and truth to tell, that very first *Maverick* tale was really a re-make of the Flynns' movie.

That's why Jim wore Flynn's wardrobe. 'Because,' he explains, 'they used stock footage from the movie for my long-shots...so I had to match my clothes to his!'

In other words, one of the rather better kept secrets of the tele-world is that Errol Flynn, no less, was an uncredited guest star in the first *Maverick* episode. It was him and not Jim seen walking through a Western township, seen on the horizon on foot or in saddle — in scenes clipped from his old movie. As soon as a Flynn long-shot became a close-up — why, there was smilin' Jim.

That, as they say, is the magic of movies. Television, too.

Countless other top star guests could be glimpsed in those early days of the classic series. 'Practically all the first *Maverick* scripts were re-writes of old Warner Brothers' pictures,' adds Jim.

It was not long, of course, before Garner and the powers that were at Warner Brothers realised their new star needed more real live help. A sidekick...'mebbe a brother,'

someone suggested...to help ease the pressure on the series' solo star.

For example, when that first episode went on the air on September 22, 1957 (it's Garner supplying these dates; like most actors, he has an uncanny memory for such incidental intelligence), only that first show was in the can. Making each *Maverick* hour took six working days. Seven days were really required, so the toil was tough. Ten minutes film in the can each day is going it some; on a movie, directors are lucky if they get four minutes shot a day. Which is the how and the why of Jack Kelly entering the series as Bret's brother Bart...to help spread the work load.

And then, of course, by the time James Garner quit the series in 1961, another member of the clan was introduced. The brothers' British cousin, Beau...played by a certain Roger Moore.

Without Jim Garner, however, the series plain fizzled out.

So indeed did the whole idea of telly-Westerns. So, indeed, did the Western itself. It died of over-exposure.

The public were bored stiff with the West. So were the studios. It wasn't until Sergio Leone and other Italians got into the act, filling the vacancy with their own spirited spaghetti Westerns — the best of which just happened to feature a tall, rangy TV cowpoke called Clint Eastwood — that new life and interest was renewed in the genre.

Back in the late '50s, though, cowboys were riding all over the tele-range. Good. Bad. And downright ugly. Jim Garner recalls there being about seventeen other cowboys on the tube when he first borrowed Errol Flynn's old clobber. In America, you could hardly twirl

the TV dial through fifteen or more channels without coming upon yet another cowpuncher being punched, shot, kissed or riding off into the sunset as (usually) Frankie Laine sang the series' theme song.

There was big Clint Walker — a hit as *Cheyenne* (Garner appeared in the very first episode). Ty Hardin was *Bronco; Will Hutchins was Sugarfoot.* Hugh O'Brien made a fortune being *Wyatt Earp,* so Gene Barry tried his luck as *Bat Masterson.*

John Lupton starred in a series based on a James Stewart Western, *Broken Arrow.* Peter Breck leapt into *The Black Saddle. Robert Culp* (better, much better later on in *I Spy*) headlined *Trackdown.* Veteran Scott Brady tried his luck as *Shotgun Slade.*

Some of the shows made instant international names of their new found stars...Steve McQueen hit the big time as bounty hunter Josh Randall in *Wanted: Dead or Alive* and Clint Eastwood stood out of the *Rawhide* crowd as Rowdy Yates. And then, who can forget the late Richard Boone's wondrous Paladin character in *Have Gun, Will Travel* which added a little sagebrush philosophy to the West and like McQueen's show had the considerable virtue of never outstaying its welcome — it filled just 25 minutes a week. Very choice minutes.

For each new star there were scores that never made it. Their skeletons must be still out there, whitened by the sun in the desert someplace.

Top of the family cluster was *Bonanza,* in which the patrician, white-haired Lorne Greene ran as tight a Ponderosa ranch as he did later with *Battlestar Galactica* and now *Code Red.* He ruled the roost with three strapping sons as his roosters.

The late Dan Blocker as the mighty Hoss, Pernell Roberts (now, the star of *Trapper John MD*) and everyone's pet, Little Joe — alias Michael Landon, the originator and star of *Little House on the Prairie.*

Anything a white-haired father figure could do, so could a white-thatched mother. And so Barbara Stanwyck won greater fame than in all her 35 years in Hollywood movies, by becoming boss of *The Big Valley,* in 1965. Her brood included Lee Majors in his first television work.

For a long while, though, certainly until *Maverick* got rolling every Sunday night, *the* No. 1. tele-Western was *Wagon Train* starring Ward Bond.

After Bond died in 1960, another film veteran, John McIntire took over the role of wagonmaster Seth Adams. For the youngsters, the real star of the show was Robert Horton — as the train's chief scout, Flint McCullough. When Horton left the show, Robert Fuller from *Laramie,* became the scout.

In all, there were 227 episodes made of *Wagon Train* — more than 200 hours.

But not even *Wagon Train,* however, could outreach the multitudinous amount of *Gunsmoke* stories. The adventures of big James Arness, aka. Marshall Matt Dillon, were surrounded by what became an increasingly soap-opera bunch of Westerners: Milburn Stone's Doc Adams; Amanda Blake's saloon wench, Kitty, and Dennis Weaver's limpalong, Chester. In all, the show lasted an incredible twenty years on the CBS network in America. A total of no less than 361 hours of gunsmokin' exploits.

With all of this TV western background it's no wonder that when James Garner was first asked to play Bret Maverick, he said: thank you — but no thanks!

Above: Clint Eastwood who first came to the public's attention as Rowdy Yates in the *Rawhide* series, has now established himself as a true international star. Here he is seen in a shot from the film *'The Outlaw Josey Wales'*.

'I didn't particularly want to play a cowboy,' he explains. 'But being under contract I hadn't much option. They were planning to put it on at a key time — I would have preferred to have it begin somewhere quietly and let it build up. Also, I couldn't help thinking that while a successful TV series can make an actor, a flop series can ruin him.'

He didn't have to fret very long. *Maverick* opened directly in competition with American television's highest rated shows and won. Maverick also saw the end of many other tele-cowpokers.

The rival shows, as Garner termed them, were full of steely-eyed heroes. He wasn't interested in joining that pack. From the outset, he tried to make *Maverick* different. He injected comedy into the show. 'No,' he counters, 'not comedy. I don't do comedy. I do *humour.'*

He was helped in this aim by the director of the first three shows, Budd Boetticher.

'He started injecting little bitty pieces of humour into the series almost immediately,' recalls Jim. Garner liked Budd's style and started suggesting ideas of his own. He remembers a big fight scene required for one early show — with only an hour to shoot it in. That's not long. Movie fights need to be choreographed as precisely as a ballet in order to make them look good on any screen, big or small.

The fight, as per script, was one of those ripe, royal John Wayne stand-up set-tos. Punch after punch until both guys could hardly stand. Garner spied some tall reeds on the location and suggested to Boetticher they shoot the tussle in the reeds — with nothing being seen of the bodies or blows except for a head or some limbs being occasionally knocked into view. The result was hilarious.

'After that we tended to use a lot of humour whenever we were pressed for time,' comments Garner. 'After three shows, the writers started putting the humour on paper and well, it just took off.'

Now after 25 years he's back. Why?

He's as honest as usual about the reasons why. 'I couldn't find anything else that interested me,' he says. 'I mean, I've done a detective — so has everyone else — and doctors are dead and lawyers have been run into the ground, and besides, neither of those two professions is too admirable at the moment. And I don't deal in futuristic things.'

He started musing on a plan to revue *Maverick* again before winding up *Rockford,* and before Warner Brothers beat him to it by deciding on the (short-lived) *Young Maverick* series in 1979. The series didn't take off, so, the way was free to bring back Bret, his way, and via his new company, Comanche.

'I started thinking what Bret would be like twenty years later,' he says, 'and what the series would look like updated from the 1860's to the 1880's. If I couldn't find a new format, I said I'd like to to like to try *Maverick* and the minute I voiced that, everybody seemed to say "Hooray! Wonderful!" and we soon couldn't get our minds on anything but Maverick.'

He had but one proviso. He couldn't carry the entire show himself. The new version would need plenty of other characters. 'I'm just not physically able to be on the screen one hour every week,' he explains. '*Rockford* really fixed that for me. I can't remember ever being in such bad shape as when I left that series. I'm a lot healthier now…but I'm not planning to be on the screen every minute.'

When he is, though, the ole Maverick magic is as good as ever. And that's the best news of this television year!

Texas Rangers of the 1880s armed with Winchesters & revolvers.

URE GALLERY

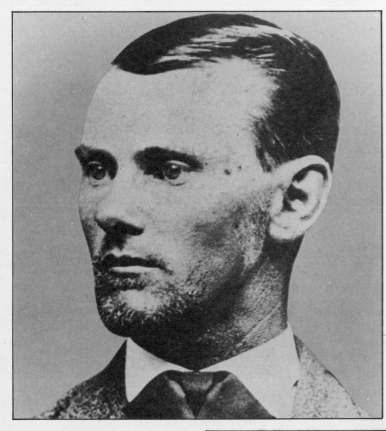

Jesse James the outlaw photographed in 1875, aged 28.

Belle Starr. "Queen of the Outlaws", with badman Blue Duck.

"Fifty dollars!" growled One-Eyed Simpson across the poker table, tugging at the stubble on his chin nervously,"...and let's see what you've got, Maverick!"

"You *sure* about this, One-Eye?" queried Maverick gently, counting out five ten-dollar bills and throwing them into the pot. "That's all you've got left..."

"Sure I'm sure!" Simpson barked shortly, a brittle, nervous edge to his voice, reaching up to adjust the patch over his left eye. Bret tried hard to suppress a smile, knowing full well that Simpson had two perfectly good eyes, just like everyone else. It was only his intelligence that was lacking, it seemed, for Simpson was a small time crook who wore the patch as a disguise, only taking it off when he was about to commit a robbery...on the idea that the victim would describe his attacker as having two good eyes. It was a sort of reverse psychology that made Simpson think he was the greatest criminal genius ever: other bandits put on masks to commit crimes...he took his off. Heaven alone knew what damage he was doing to his eye, keeping it covered up all the time...

Another thing Simpson lacked, apart from brains, was any sense of how to play poker. He was the perfect sucker, and it had taken Bret about five minutes to realise that every time Simpson was unsure of his hand, he'd nervously reach up and adjust the eye-patch. Still, if he wanted to throw his money away at cards, that was his lookout. Bret laid down his Royal Flush and started to reach for the pot.

Simpson's eye bulged in horror for a moment as he goggled at the picture cards, and then he throw in his hand face down and got suddenly to his feet, knocking over his chair.

"You no good, low-down, side-winding, cheating son of a..." began Simpson loudly and angrily, reaching for his holster and then realising that the house rules of the Red Ox saloon had compelled him to check his gun at the door.

"Language! Language!" chided Bret, barely able to restrain a chuckle and pointing to the door of the saloon, where the Reverend Jones could be seen, just entering and holding a collecting box. Simpson turned to look, paused for a moment, then turned back to Bret, his anger still boiling, his fists bunching.

"Don't try and smart-talk me, Maverick!" he shouted, shoving the table aside and advancing on Bret, fists raised. A heavy hand settled on his shoulder.

"Outside, Simpson!" said Tom Guthrie coldly, turning the angry loser round. Simpson, snarling through the gaps in his teeth, started to swing a punch, then thought better of it as he saw Guthrie's hand drop to his hip. As the owner, Tom Guthrie was the only man allowed to wear a gun on the premises.

"I run a clean house here, and you know it!" Guthrie continued. *Nobody* cheats here!"

"Nobody but *him*!" yelled Simpson, pointing at Bret. "You got rules for everyone else...but *he* owns half the place as well!"

"Rules is rules," explained Guthrie, looking round at the other customers of the Red Ox, who had paused in their gaming and drinking to watch the confrontation. "Anyone around here think they've ever seen Bret Maverick cheating?"

Bret smiled with satisfaction at the silence which greeted this question. Simpson could only stamp his foot in frustration.

"If you lose, you lose..." Guthrie told him, his hand still hovering threateningly about the butt of his gun. "Now get out..."

"Eight hundred dollars..." muttered Simpson to no one in particular, hunched his shoulders and stomped toward the door, shoving aside Reverend Jones as he went. A normal babble of conversation returned to the Red Ox as Guthrie straightened the table and sat down next to Maverick, who was now gathering up his winnings.

"Maybe it ain't such a good idea, cleaning out the suckers like that, Bret..." said Guthrie, smiling wearily. "Maybe you should let'em win the last hand...just so they've got a little cash to go home with..."

"Hell, Tom, I already let him win three 'last hands'," Bret smiled, "but what can you do? As soon as you give a sucker a break, they think they've hit a lucky streak, and want to go right on playing. Eventually, you've just got to take their money..."

"Yeah, I guess you're right," agreed Guthrie morosely, eyeing the Reverend Jones as he started going round the tables with his collecting box, with varying success.

"What I can't understand," Bret continued, "is where a know-nothing turkey like Simpson gets eight hundred dollars?"

"Robbery..." came the obvious answer. "A little here, a little there. A stagecoach, a liquor store, ordinary folks out walking...happens every day. Simpson operates over the state-line, then crosses back to spend his money here. The crooks around Sweetwater do the same thing, but they head in the opposite direction..."

"You mean..." Bret began in mock horror, starting to pocket his winnings, "all this money's *stolen?*"

"Probably," shrugged Guthrie, "but you won it fair and square, so..."

"Ahem...excuse me, gentlemen...interrupted the soft, nervous voice of the Reverend Jones, and they looked up to see the preacher running a hand through his thin white hair.

"Evening, Reverend," said Guthrie affably. "Don't often see you in a den of iniquity like this!"

The preacher looked even more uncomfortable than ever, then sat down abruptly and began to babble hurriedly: "No, it's not my favourite place, but dire necessity forces me to seek for charity wherever I can find it. I'm collecting for the church roofing fund you see...and I'm afraid that for the last two weeks running, some miserable sinner has stolen the collection money at the Sunday services! It amounts to several dollars!''

"Disgusting!" growled Guthrie, reaching into his pocket for a silver dollar. Bret looked down at his eight hundred dollars; paused, shrugged, and then threw four tens into the collecting box. Reverend Jones' face lit up.

"Good night...muttered Bret, and then got up

hurriedly before the preacher could pour out his thanks. He headed for the door, but Guthrie called him back and took him aside.

"Bank doesn't open until tomorrow," Guthrie explained, "and if I were you, I'd be kinda worried, carrying eight hundred or so

around in the dark. Why don't you leave it in the safe overnight?"

"Guess you're right, Tom," agreed Bret, handing over the money before he headed out of the Red Ox, mounted Lo-Ball, and rode off in the direction of the Lazy Ace.

He didn't get far. Not much farther than the edge of town.

Bret knew he was going to be robbed when he found he could see no sign of the eye-patch. "Hello, Simpson," he said wearily, raising his arms.

Simpson twitched angrily, though his gun remained trained on Bret's chest. He didn't like it when someone saw through his 'disguise', though he had to admit it had been happening more and more frequently recently. "Search him!" he hissed, and two more men rode out of the shadows, revolvers in their hands.

Bret sat there patiently while Dog-face Charley and Zeke Zimmer searched him, removing the derringer from his sleeve, felt in his pockets and opened his jacket. They turned toward Simpson and shook their heads.

"Where's my eight hundred dollars?" growled One-Eye Simpson, riding closer.

"You mean *my* eight hundred dollars," Bret corrected him quietly. Locked up in Tom Guthrie's safe back at the Red Ox. Forget it, fellas...there's no way you're going to get it..."

"That's what *you* think, Maverick!" spat Simpson, both eyes glinting angrily. "Bring him along with us..."

Half an hour's ride under a silver-sickle moon brought them to a tumbledown cabin in the hills, which obviously hadn't had any reasonably civilised inhabitants for years. The musty-smelling, ruinous interior only confirmed the first impression; the place was little better than an animal pen. Just the right place for One-Eye Simpson and Dog-face Charley, thought Bret as they led him within.

Zeke Zimmer uncorked a bottle of red-eye as Simpson and Charley sat Bret down on a ricketty wooden chair, tied his ankles to the chair-legs, and his left hand to the back.

"Haven't you forgotten something, fellas?" remarked Bret, waving his right hand pointedly.

"Shut up, wise-guy!" said Simpson, now replacing his eye-patch and dragging a table closer. Bret noticed with wry amusement that it only had three and half legs.

"Now, we're going to play us a little poker," announced Simpson, pulling a chair to the opposite side of the table, and producing a dog-eared deck of cards. "Only *this* time we're playing with my deck, and you're playing one-handed. That way there ain't gonna be no cheating..."

"Whatever you say, One-Eye," aquiesced Bret, glancing round to see Charley and Zimmer pulling up stools and sitting on either side of him, their guns pointed at his head. "But what are we using for stake money? Like I said...I left all my cash back at the Red Ox..."

Simpson gave him a venomous one-eyed stare, then got up angrily and walked over to a cupboard at one side of the room, jerking the handle. The door came off and fell to the floor, throwing up a cloud of dust. With a muttered oath, Simpson pulled out a canvas money-sack and returned to the table. As he upended the sack, a pile of small silver coins poured onto the table-top.

"We're playing for nickels and dimes?" asked Bret, surprised and amused. "Tell me, Simpson, where'd you get all that small change? You haven't by any chance been robbing the collection plate at the Sweetwater Church, have you?"

"Shut your mouth!" snapped Simpson, his face reddening as he divided the coins into two roughly equal piles and pushed one toward Bret. "Now, listen, Maverick, the way we're playing is this..." He picked up a ten cent piece and thrust it toward Bret's face. "Every time *you* lose one of these, it costs you ten dollars. Every time *I* lose one, it costs me a dime! Fair?"

"Fair?!" ejaculated Bret, then glanced round at the gun-barrels trained on his temples. "Sure..." he agreed. "You'll have to deal, though. Unless you want to untie my other hand?"

"Shut up!" said Simpson, and they settled down to play cards.

An hour passed. An hour that saw much eye-patch adjusting from Simpson, and several winces of anguish from Zeke Zimmer and Dog-face Charley. And then it was all over.

"So what now, Simpson?" asked Bret, glancing down at the large pile of coins in front of him and the empty table in front of his opponent.

"Shut up!" shouted Simpson, unable to think of anything more imaginative. He got up and went to stare moodily out of the glassless window.

"We've still got Maverick!" remarked Simpson after several minutes thinking. "We could send Guthrie a ransom note...Maverick for our eight hundred dollars..."

"Uh...only one problem there, One-Eye..." stammered Charley. "I mean, Zeke and I never learned no letters, and you...you..."

"Alright," said Bret wearily. "*I'll* write your ransom note. You got any paper? A pencil?"

After another fifteen minutes searching, Bret was finally provided with a dead matchstick and the back of a Chinese laundry bill to write on. "Now, what do you want to say?"

Another long pause, and then Simpson announced: "Say...Guthrie, if you ever want to see that mangy rat of a partner of yours alive, bring eight hundred dollars to Big Oak Hill tomorrow...no, we won't be delivering the note

till the morning...make that today...at noon. And don't make no trouble.''

Bret sat there and dutifully wrote the note, then handed it over to Simpson, who looked at it uncomprehendingly and handed it to Zeke Zimmer. Then, leaving Bret still tied to the chair, but with both hands tied this time, they retired for the night.

Soon after dawn, Zimmer put the note in an empty bourbon bottle and headed for town. Half an hour later, he was back, looking pleased with himself.

"Well?" asked Simpson. "Did you deliver it?"

"Sure...threw the bottle through the front window and headed straight back here. No one on my tail, either..."

"The front window?" Bret groaned. "Do you guys know how much window-glass costs these days?"

"Shut up!" said Simpson, reaching out for an over-brewed coffee-pot on the stove, then leaping back with a curse as the handle burnt his hand.

At half past ten, the cabin door suddenly burst open, and Tom Guthrie strode in, gun in hand, with three other men from Sweetwater at his back. Zeke Zimmer went for his gun, and got a bullet in his shoulder for his trouble. Dog-faced Charley

started to run for the back door, then thought better of it as a bullet whistled past his ear. One-Eye Simpson gave up with a fight.

"How'd you find us, Guthrie?" asked Simpson as one of the townsmen started untying Bret.

"It was pretty easy..." grinned Guthrie, throwing a loop of rope round Simpson's wrists. "That note from Bret told us exactly where to find him..."

"You mean...you didn't write what I told you?" asked Simpson, looking toward Bret with undisguised loathing.

"Would you?" asked Bret in reply, standing up and rubbing his wrists.

"I always knew you were a cheat, Maverick!" yelled Simpson.

"And I always knew you were a sucker, One-Eye!" replied Bret, going over to the doorless cupboard and pulling out the sack of small change. Handing it to one of his rescuers, he said: "Here, give this to Reverend Jones...tell him an anonymous donor decided to contribute to the church roofing fund..."

"I'll kill you for this, Maverick!" shouted Simpson as his captors led him away.

"Shut up..." remarked Bret, and went looking for his horse...

Fade-in…

The scene: Columbia Pictures' studios at 1,438 North Gower Street, Hollywood. The wrong side of the Hollywood tracks — what the smug tycoons like Louis B. Mayer and Jack Warner at MGM and Warner Brothers used to denigrate as Poverty Row.

The year: 1953.

The players: A veteran Columbia talent coach, Benno Schneider. And a young, nervous — 'scared to death' — 25-year-old ex-G.I. wanderer from Oklahoma, name of James Bumgarner.

The reason: Although completely untrained as an actor, the younger man was having a reading — an audition — on the advice and indeed, the last time they'd met was when Jim was filling cars with Shell petrol at a service station on Hollywood Boulevard. One of his customers was Paul Gregory, then a lowly soda jerk, behind the counter of the Gotham Drug Store, up the road a piece.

A little diversion known historically as the Korean War separated them. When Jim returned to Hollywood (where his father lived and worked in the carpet business), he found himself driving past the La Brea Avenue building with a notice on it saying: Paul Gregory and Associates. Jim decided to look in. He was, as most people do in Los Angeles, thinking about being an actor. He'd see what Paul thought. It was now or never.

'Here's the part where fate steps in,' grins Garner. 'See, if I get an urge to do something but it's not convenient to do it, I won't. Well, there was a parking space in front of Paul's building — and if that space hadn't been there, I would never have driven around the block to look for one.'

He went in. Talked about his plans for an hour or more with his old buddy. 'Look at yourself, Jim,' said Paul, 'and hear what you sound like. There's definitely a chance that something could happen if you learned how to act.'

He didn't change his mind, either, when hearing about Benno Schneider's instant review of his friend's chances. Paul Gregory was putting

THE JAMES GARNER PROFILE

recommendation of an old pal turned showbiz agent and producer. 'I wasn't looking for stardom,' recalls the would-be actor. 'I was looking for a job. Something I could make a living at.'

The verdict: After the reading, Schneider looks Bumgarner up and down and doesn't waste too much time about it. 'I don't know what you've been doing, young man,' said the talent expert, 'but you really should go back to it. Just because you're young doesn't mean you can be an actor.'

Fade out.

Well, not quite. More than one superstar career has been founded on ill-advised comments like that. Although in the case of the man who became James Garner, the verdict was probably very true. At the time.

Fortunately, for Jim, his pal, Paul Gregory did not agree. The

together a Broadway play at the time — *The Caine Mutiny Court Martial* with Henry Fonda, Lloyd Nolan and John Hodiak. Before hitting New York, the play, and its strong Hollywood rather than Broadway names, would go on a tour around America. Paul gave Jim a job. His start as an actor.

It was a novel beginning. James Garner didn't say a word on stage for a full year…!

He played one of the six judges who sat on a dais listening to all the evidence in the play's trial — and said not one line of dialogue. Yet as Garner has said more than once, it was a helluva good way to begin. He learnt his trade by watching the show's stars — masters at their profession — every night for a year.

They seemed to take to him

as well. He later became John Hodiak's understudy, Lloyd Nolan taught him about concentration and, well, after twelve months on the same stage as the great Henry Fonda, if you don't learn something about acting — such as to stay in it or quit — he shouldn't really have been on the stage in the first place. 'What I really learned from him was a professional attitude and concentration.'

Soon after the play ended its Broadway run (during which time the noviate actor had turned down a screen-test from 20th Century Fox in New York), Paul Gregory had another job for him. Same play, different job. For the new post-Broadway tour, Garner was given a proper speaking role. This time, too, the piece was being directed by the noted screen star Charles Laughton. And it was the late, great British actor who gave the young Garner, perhaps the best advice of his life.

'Your problem, Jim,' diagnosed Laughton, 'is you're afraid to be bad.'

'He was absolutely right, of course,' agrees Garner. New as he was to the acting business, James Garner was still fighting his childhood fear of performing — plays, songs, anything - in public. Of maybe making a complete ass of himself. He was trying so hard not to be bad, he left himself little time to try and be good.

As we all know, he dropped his defences and learned. After four months touring the court martial play in Texas, Louisiana, Arkansas and his home state of Oklahoma, Garner's next job was…a Winston cigarette commercial. He got the words wrong, there, too, but no matter. The fee financed him for the eight months until he finally cracked his first movie and won himself a Warner Brothers movie contract. Three films later and something called *Maverick* rolled along…

His was a rapid rise for a fellow who had never seemed to know where he was going in life. Jim Garner was born in a town called Norman, in Oklahoma.

His father ran a country store just out of town. Jim's mother died when he was five and together with his two elder brothers he was raised by a stepmother who had a thing about punishing wrongs, supposed and otherwise, with thwacks from sticks, boards, spatulars — whatever she had in her hand.

'She had this thing about whipping,' Garner told Playboy magazine. 'She used to make us go out and cut willow switches and then she'd beat us on the butt with them.'

Jim almost left home before she did and by 14 had won his chauffeur's licence and became a driving salesman for a clothes company. That was the first of numerous jobs over the ten

years before parking his car outside Paul Gregory' office building.

'Oh, I must have held approximately fifty jobs or more in my time,' Garner admits. 'Never stayed in anything or anywhere longer than three or four months. I just went whichever way the wind blew. I've been a waiter, lifeguard, hod-carrier on a building site, dish-washer, window decorator, grocery clerk, insurance salesman, gas station attendant. I've swamped trucks — that's loading and unloading 'em. I was a roughneck in the Texas and Oklahoma oil-fields. Then, when I was at Hollywood High School, I earned 15 bucks an hour modelling swimsuits for the Jantzen people for three days in

Palm Springs. Hah, I was even a golfball retriever one time…'

Not to mention being janitor at the University of Oklahoma. He did that to support himself when returning to Norman and attending the high school there. He'd gone back mainly to play (American) football for the school. But he dropped out — what else? — at 16 and joined the Merchant Marines in New Orleans. That lasted a year or so. Then he was back in Oklahoma, joining the State National Guard for a spell, before returning to live with his father in Los Angeles, pumping petrol, meeting Paul Gregory and getting a letter from Uncle Sam. He'd become Oklahoma's first military draftee into the Korean conflict.

That took care of his wanderlust for 14 months — and very nearly his life. When he left the Army in June 1952, he'd been awarded two Purple Hearts for being wounded in action with the Fifth Regimental Combat Team of the 24th Division. The first time was on his second day in Korea — the second was far more serious.

'That's when I was wounded by *my own side!* he exclaims. 'It happened when I got separated from my outfit because of a barrage attack on the Chinese positions. I dove for cover. But the planes from our Navy, taking me and a young South Korean boy for Red Chinese, let us have it with 20mm rockets. When they hit, they spray white phosphorous in all directions. And that stuff *burns*! I got badly burned on my backside but managed to walk the eight miles to our lines. When I got to hospital, my knees had swollen up like balloons.'

That, as he found out back home was the end of his footballing. He studied this time at the Oklahoma University, instead of cleaning it. He took a business administration course. Typically enough, he quit after a single term. That's when he started living in L.A. again, laying carpets for his father…and calling on Paul Gregory.

His first three films at Warner Brothers were nothing much to shout about: seven minutes in a William Holden movie; very much second fiddle to Tab Hunter, of all forgotten people, in a Natalie Wood romance; and Randolph Scott's sidekick in an *el cheapo* Western. All the same, Garner found himself on the threshold of stardom when the studio decided to make a love story set in post-war Japan, *Sayonara*...goodbye in Japanese.

The producer's dream casting for the American officer and his Tokyo lady-love was Marlon Brando and Audrey Hepburn. Too expensive, even in 1957! The next idea was more flexible. Either Brando and a Japanese actress — or Audrey Hepburn and an unknown American. Jim Garner, in fact.

But it was not to be. Director Joshua Logan went for Brando and Miiko Taka. And it was *sayonara,* Jim!

Not quite. There was another role he could fill in the film: Brando's officer buddy. However, another unknown, John Smith, was being considered for that...until Garner fought for it. As Garner told the film-makers, John Smith would cost them $1,200 a week. But as a Warners' contract player in a Warners' movie, Jim would only have to be paid his weekly $250 dollars.

That, of course, was exactly the kind of language any Hollywood producer understood. *Sayonara,* John!

Jim got the part and still talks with awe of the treat of working and learning from the mighty Brando. All the same, Garner probably regretted his bargaining. He's sure he only won the *Maverick* show, because he was considered cheap enough by Warner TV.

Paradoxically, Garner won his next movie because the chosen star, Charlton Heston, quit after a financial row. Garner took over the lead in *The Young Invaders.* He was too young for the role at 29, but it meant his salary rose to $500 a week and he needed it. His wife, Lois, was

expecting their daughter, Gigi, and Lois's daughter from her first marriage, Kimberly, was just out of hospital after being struck with polio at eight.

And so, James Garner had made it. He'd become a star. No one was more surprised than the 'dumb cowboy' as he referred to himself. 'When I grew up,' he explains, 'I went to cowboy movies like everyone else. But I never really wanted to be an actor. I just wanted a job. Wal, the truth is I wanted to be wealthy!'

Given the strictures of the small print in Hollywood studio contracts of the '50s, that was not necessarily that easy. When *Maverick* was earning millions around the globe, the star had won another rise. He was now

getting all of 1,250 dollars a week. No wonder he was getting tired of the tube. 'If you have any pride in your work, you don't go on TV,' he used to say. 'If you want to sell underarm deodorant, that's what you do!'

Well, yes, he was bitter.

Jim was learning the harsher, financial facts of an actor's life, as rapidly as he was mastering his thespian trade. Although he spent a single term only on that 'varsity business admin. course, he's proved a whizz at business. He may complain about the little money he earns, yet he's siphoned it off into banking, a national chain of garages. He's a director in several oil companies and a partner in a multi-million dollar apartment complex in Palo Alto,

California. He also has his film/TV production companies: Cherokee which made *The Rockford Files* and several films, and Comanche which makes *Bret Maverick* for his old studio, Warner Brothers.

As an actor, he never priced himself out of the market. He kept his salary down, while other TV runaway stars hiked their salaries into the millions. From the outset, though, he always fought for a reasonable cut of the profits of his films and TV series. He felt, quite rightly, it was his due. The fact that he didn't win his way with Maverick, is the reason he quit the series in 1961 and returned to movies.

After his mainly war movies with Warner Brothers, Garner moved away into film dramas, comedies, a touch of espionage and private detection and, yes, every so often, a return to his Maverickish images — Westerns. He's made all kinds of horse-operas — from spaghetti Westerns to Disney family Westerns (one dealing with camels, and the other set on a Hawaii cattle ranch). He's played Wyatt Earp and followed Humphrey Bogart into the gumshoes of Philip Marlowe.

He has made a virtue out of cowardice — or at least being, continually, anti-heroic. As he said right from the start of *Maverick.* 'I can't stand steely-eyed sheriffs. Bravery bores me.' His line in heroes, therefore, from Maverick to Rockford, from the 'dog robber' (con-man) in *The Americanisation of Emily,* his favourite movie, to his Texas wheeler-dealer in *Separate Beds,* all tend to behave much as his audience does. They look after No. 1 and when, and if necessary, help out anyone who needs assistance they find in their path.

He does it all with such great, winning aplomb. But then he always did, way back as a kid when a girlfriend called Betty Jane Smith (what else?) nicknamed him Slick. There is, though, nothing slick about his work. He's not flashy. He's thorough. He's good. And very real. True. Honest. One of us…

'Jim's under-rated and unique,' says Meta Rosenberg, executive producer on all his TV series. 'He's got intelligence, humour and charm. And he can make the audience feel that he's saying things naturally — just as they occur to him.'

Although his films have covered the dramatic waterfront from psychological drama *(36 Hours, Woman Without A Face)* to having the time of his life belting formula-one cars around European tracks for *Grand Prix* (when the film's insurance company found out about that, they cancelled Garner's insurance-cover for the shooting), Garner's movies are best known, loved and remembered for their humour.

He's at his best in light comedy — very much a Cary Grant, Oklahoma style. Like Grant, he says, 'Humour is much more subtle than comedy.'

The humorous side of Garner surfaced as easily as his *Cash McCall* film in 1960, blossomed opposite the perfect Tony Randall in *Boys' Night Out* and really took off when Jim made a brace of movies with Doris Day. Who can forget, for example, *The Thrill Of It All?* And the *amazing* look on Dr. Garner's face when he drove his 1958 Chevvy convertible back home…and straight into a swimming pool that had not been there when he left for work in the morning…!

That's a classic moment equalling anything put over by Cary Grant or Rock Hudson, Doris Day's other best partners.

'You can't miss with a girl like Doris,' Garner has praised. 'I'd rather have her in a film than Elizabeth Taylor. Doris is quite a girl. Working with her is a ball. I heard she was ''temperamental'', but I never saw any proof of that. It's all nonsense. The trouble is that too much that is written about Doris is not true. She was supposed to be ''different'', too, because she doesn't drink, smoke or go to parties. Well, I've never been a Hollywood party man myself -what's wrong with that?'

In Hollywood circles, Jim is, in fact, as much a loner as most of his screen heroes are, and rarely gives interviews. 'I can't help that,' he says. 'I'm not a joiner-in. I like to be independent. Always have been. I've looked after myself since I was fourteen. My real friends recognise I'm that way and it doesn't bother them.

'Oh, I'm a good enough mixer once you get me — force me out. Getting me to go out in the first place is the problem! I get a lot of invites from motion picture companies to premiers and cocktail parties. That's just not me. If I go out, I don't want to be pitched on somebody's new book or movie. I don't happen to like what people call cocktail parties, where people stand around talking about nothing. Me? I'm always looking for a place to sit down. I prefer to be comfortable. That's why I hire public relations people — to keep people *away* from me, not to get me publicity.'

His second film with Doris Day was *Move Over, Darling,* and it's this film that Garner remembers best.

'I ought to,' he winces. 'I broke one of her ribs in that film. During the scene where Doris fights with Polly Bergen, I had to separate them…that's when it happened. And I know how a broken rib can hurt, because I busted one in a movie once. But, as far as Doris was concerned, everything went on as normal. She acted as if nothing had happened. She turned up the next day, happy and smiling, despite the pain and special bandages. Now, does that sound like a temperamental star to you?'

Garner knows about the pain of more than busted ribs. He says he was in his worst physical shape by the time he quit opening *The Rockford Files* in 1980. TV fans have little idea about the strain of making a top TV series — mental and physical. A star like Garner, for instance, is shooting five, often six days a week, non-stop for four or five months at a stretch.

Making in fact, almost the equivalent of a new movie every ten days. At that kind of rapid pace, the odd slip, trip or slide can easily happen — and just can't be allowed to interfere with schedules unless hospitalisation is urgently required.

Totalling his injuries accrued during three breakneck TV series, Garner can list knee operations, busted ribs and knuckles, torn ligaments and tendons, disintergrated discs in his back and so on. His worst, longest complaint is his knees — never in good shape since Korea. He's broken his right kneecap twice in the same place and has had some five surgical incisions made into it. 'The last time, they went in with a hammer and chisel to see if they could get it to bend more than 100 degrees.' As one of his doctors told him. 'Your knee is fine. For a man of 85!'

His film career was slipping into something of the perennial decline until he went back to television as ex-con turned private investigator, Jim Rockford in 1974. A slow-burning hit from the opening TV-movie, the Rockford character owed much to Garner's performance in the *Marlowe* film. The series was allowed the rare luxury of building up from a tepid beginning to top of the ratings.

Although varying generations of international TV viewers have fallen for the Garner magic in the old *Maverick* or the more recent *Rockford* shows, James Garner feels his very best TV series is the one that go way…*Nichols,* born and died in 1971. This ran for 26 episodes only, a single season in American television parlance. Jim's turn-of-the century sheriff character was greatly inspired by his two delightful, rib-tickling Western send-up movies, also produced by his own Cherokee company: *Support Your Local Sheriff* and the follow up, *Support Your Local Gunfighter.*

Critics did not, however, take so kindly to the new tele-sheriff. 'A terrible waste of

Garner,' said Variety, the Showbiz Bible. 'Vague, often silly and often unsympathetic.' However, *Nichols* won some fans. Critic Rochelle Reed felt it was a warming, charming show. 'There's a lot that could be said in criticism by spoil-sports: too over-produced, too limp, too cornball. But the wide-eyed unsophistication of James Garner turns it all round…'

'I still think,' sums up Jim, 'that *Nichols* is the best of the three TV series I've done. Only 18 of the 26 shows were ever seen in America, but I really think the show was five or ten years ahead of its time, it drew a pretty fine line between making social comment and being entertaining.'

What kind of hero was *Nichols?* 'Maverick and *Rockford* were pretty much alike as characters, but *Nichols* — he was a whole different kinda bird.'

It's odds on that certain areas which Garner liked to investigate in the *Nichols* format, will work themselves into his grand, spanking all-new *Bret Maverick* shows. Our lovable gamblin' man is not quite at the turn of the century West yet — more in the 1880s. But the opportunity for social comment is there, in his rich group of new characters in Sweetwater, Arizona.

The new *Maverick* show could also bring back more of the West to the box in the corner…though as Hollywood well knows, Jim Garner is a hard act to beat.

When his original *Maverick* show hit the tube in 1957, television was already glutted with cowboys. Each and every saddle-sore series kept trying to ape, or at least keep up with their rivals. The same mindless, copy-cat moves we saw repeated time and time again in more recent years with the interminable cop shows. In both instances, cowpokes and cops, one star alone stood out head, shoulders and *wit* above the average, rinky-dink repitition of characters and scripts.

That star was and still is

James Garner — whether as Bret Maverick or Jim Rockford.

For all his movies — and he's made as many flops as the next man — Jim Garner remains the ultimate, definitive TV star. Someone we never want to miss each week. His good looks, and what he can do with them — wondrous low-key expressions of humour, annoyance, pain and sheer whimsicality — seem better attuned to the small screen than the large. Maybe, he simply *seems* more at home on our home screens because that's where most of us first met him. And that was so long ago now, he's become almost one of the family. And he aims to remain so for quite a few years yet. Just as long as he doesn't have to talk about it…please.

'I'm a guy who likes to be left alone — especially when I'm not working,' he agrees. 'Remember when I am working I'm at it for 14 hours a day, so when I finish I want to get off and hide away and do mah thing.'

He once carried his privacy concerns to the extent of bribing the maker of those tourist maps of the Hollywood stars' homes — to leave his name and address off the map listings. Any fan that did find his home rarely found Jim. 'My daughter, Gigi, usually knows how to handle them,' he laughs. 'She says something like: 'Oh, you don't wanna see him — he's the meanist old thing!'

His fan mail gets answered, of course, but he doesn't like all the compliments he gets in them — or from other people about his work, which just happens to be the best in American TV series. 'I can't accept praise for one reason or another,' he says. 'I feel either that such compliments are not deserved or that I can't fully believe them.'

Why then, is he an actor at all, one wonders?

'I'm in movies and television because I enjoy the work,' he comments. 'I enjoy being there on the set, acting in front of the camera and all the other things that go with that. In fact, after the real pleasure of doing a show with a really good production crew, I don't really care whether it gets on the air or not.

'The way I look at it is that show business is an honest way of making a living. I don't know any other job that would pay me as much as this — and I've tried plenty! The thing is not to take yourself too seriously. Do that as an actor — and you're inviting trouble.

'But, yeah, sure, anybody can become an actor with a little luck. I mean, I don't think I have any special image. There isn't any niche I want to put myself in. The critics, they say I'm a ''personality''. What I'm aiming for is the day they tab me as an ''actor''. That's all I am. An actor who always feels that his next job may well be his last.

'I'm no comic, you see. I don't do jokes. I don't come out there with a lollipop and say ''dem'' and ''dose''. I'm not…*flashy!* I'm much more interested in creating characters than being flashy. Because flash hits quick…and leaves quick. Characters go on and on.'

Better still, like *Bret Maverick,* they come back as No. 1 again.

'Hah!' snorts James Garner. 'I'm not interested in being No. 1. Nor even No. 2. I guess I've done a helluva lot better than I ever thought I would.

'Being about No. 7 is about right for me.'

WILD WEST PICTURE GALLERY

Henry 'Heck' Thomas, noted deputy U.S. Marshal who hunted down many outlaws.

Locomotive and freight cars of the Atchison, Topeka and Santa Fe Railroad at Glorieta, New Mexico, in 1880.

John Henry "Doc" Holliday was perhaps the most notorious gambler-gunfighter of the Old West. Wyatt Earp, the legendary frontier marshal, a close friend and fellow cardsharp had this to say of Holliday a few years after his death:

"Doc was a dentist whom necessity had made a gambler; a gentleman whom illness had made a frontier vagabond . . . a long, lean, ash-blond fellow nearly dead with consumption, and at the same time the most skilful gambler and the nerviest, speediest, deadliest man with a six-gun I ever knew."

Holliday may have been a qualified dentist, but he drilled more torsoes than teeth. He is credited with at least sixteen killings. To those who first met him he looked harmless enough, with his pale face, slim hands, dark clothes and bowler hat. But he always carried a gun and a bowie knife. He had cold blue eyes, a quick temper, and his short life was a succession of violent incidents.

Born in Georgia in 1852, son of a wealthy lawyer, he studied dentistry in Baltimore. At the age of 21 he developed consumption (a disease of the lungs, attended by severe coughing) and was advised to go West where the dry climate would benefit his health. He went to Texas where he killed a man in Dallas and fled. He became a heavy drinker, gave up dentistry, and earned his living as a professional gambler. He would sit at the card table coughing blood into his handkerchief as he played.

Knowing that he would surely die a young man made Doc Holliday a fatalist, not caring if he lived or died, a reckless outlook that made him a dangerous man indeed. One day in 1877 Doc sat down in Fort Griffin to play poker with a notorious character named Ed Bailey, who started sneaking looks at the discarded cards, known as the "deadwood". Doc told Bailey to stop checking the deadwood and to "play poker". When Bailey persisted and Doc stopped the game, Bailey pulled a gun. But before he could get off a shot, Doc whipped out his knife and

killed the troublemaker.

Doc became firm friends with Wyatt Earp after he saved Earp's life in a desperate situation with a bunch of cowboys in Dodge City, Kansas. When Wyatt and his brothers moved to Tombstone, Arizona, Holliday went with them and in 1881 helped out the Earps at the most celebrated shoot-out of the Old West, the Gunfight in the O.K. Corral (see feature MYTHS OF THE WEST). Six years later Doc cashed in his chips for the last time when he died in the sanitorium at Glenwood Springs, Colorado, aged 35.

Luke Short, born in Mississippi, was another noted gambler-gunman, an associate of Holliday and Earp. Short by name and short in stature, Luke stood five feet six inches tall, but he was a mean man to tangle with. Luke had a hatred of physical, menial labour. He had a mathematical mind, swift and sure where playing cards and percentages were concerned. He wandered the West and owned a succession of gambling saloons.

Luke dressed in the height of fashion and, in a rough and ready frontier society, his elegant costume invited comment. Mostly he shrugged off the joshing, but if somebody overstepped the mark he usually wished he had not. When a big loudmouth attempted to flip Luke's tophat from his head, the little gambler pulled out his revolver and knocked the man cold with the barrel, leaping in the air to do so. Luke did not shoot to kill if it could be avoided.

Another time a fellow named Brown set out deliberately to provoke Short as he played faro. Several times Brown, who was not in the game, leaned over the table and moved Luke's chips saying, "Play it that way

Gamblers

shorty." Luke was not easily baited and said nothing the first time. When Brown repeated his interference, Luke warned him to stay away. Brown stepped back, cursing, and went for his gun. Luke was faster, he shot and severely wounded the man.

Charlie Storms, another professional gambler, once threw chips into Luke's face over a losing turn of the cards. Storms was the worse for drink and Luke let the incident pass. Some years later, however, when Storms ran into Luke in Tombstone, he attempted to shoot the little gambler and got himself killed instead. Luke Short met a similar end to that of Doc Holliday, he died in bed of a sickness, aged 39.

Wild Bill Hickok was an inveterate gambler. So was the dashing General George A. Custer and Buffalo Bill Cody. With Hickok, gambling was a passion not a profession. But he sported the sartorial fashion and courteous manner in keeping with a gaming gentleman. A formidable gunfighter, Hickok was often hired as a peace officer by townships to maintain law and order. His reputation spread far and wide, much publicised by writers and journalists, who daubed him the "Prince of Pistoleers."

Born James Butler Hickok in 1837 he started his Western adventures as a stagecoach driver. It is said that he won his famous nickname "Wild Bill" when single-handed he stopped a mob from lynching a man. An impressive figure, he was over six feet tall with shoulder length hair. In 1865 he engaged professional gambler Dave Tutt in a shoot-out that established the classic gunfight encounter that served as the pattern for Western movies.

The gunfight was triggered by an argument over a game of poker. Tutt acquired Hickok's watch in the game and boasted that he would wear the timepiece as a symbol of victory in the town's square. Hickok ob-

Left: Doc Holliday, dentist turned professional gambler and gunfighter. Above: Luke Short, a dandy dresser and a dangerous man when provoked.

jected to this (for he was intent on winning it back) but Tutt ignored the warning. When the cardsharp appeared in the square flaunting the watch, Hickok confronted him at a distance of fifty yards. Both drew their pistols at the same time. Tutt missed his mark and fell dead with a bullet through the heart.

Hickok immediately turned round on Tutt's armed friends and levelled his pistol at them saying, "Aren't you satisfied gentlemen? Put up your shooting-irons, or there'll be more dead men here." Having seen enough of Hickok's cracksho ability, the men dispersed. Bil stood trial for Tutt's death bu was acquitted on his plea of sel defence.

Hickok had the habit when playing cards of making sure that he sat with his back to the wall, facing the doorway, as a precaution against being sur-

d Gunmen

prised by a gunman. It was a custom that served him well, for he had numerous enemies and there were plenty of ambitious gunslingers just waiting the opportunity to shoot him down. On an afternoon in August 1876 Hickok entered a saloon in Deadwood, Dakota Territory, and joined a poker game.

Another player was sitting in Bill's customary wall chair. Not wishing to make a fuss with people he knew, Bill took the empty chair and sat with his back to the door. A fatal lapse in his code of survival. As the

George Devol, professional gambler for forty years had the hardest head on the Mississippi River.

game progressed, a hired assassin named Jack McCall walked quietly through the door and shot Wild Bill through the back of the head. Hickok was holding the ace of spades, ace of clubs, eight of spades, eight of clubs, and the jack of diamonds: these "aces and eights" became known in poker lore as the "Deadman's Hand."

George Devol was renowned as the "hardest-headed gambler on the Mississippi." When trouble erupted over the gaming table George did not resort to gunplay, for he was a champion rough-and-tumble fighter who excelled in head-butting. In order to protect his supple hands, hard-headed George used his noggin as a battering-ram and knocked out many big men in this manner.

Born in Ohio in 1829, George Devol spent most of his life gambling on the Mississippi steamboats. Nearly six feet tall and weighing 195 pounds, he was as tough as an ox and crafty as a fox. Once, when he fleeced a Texan of 800 dollars the angry loser drew a pearl-handled gun and demanded his money back.

"Calm yourself, sir," Devol whispered to the man. "If I give you the money back at pistol point all the other losers will want their money returned also. I'll make a compromise. Bet your fine pistol against the 800 dollars and I will let you win." The Texan agreed and money and pistol were placed with a stakeholder. Devol had the winning hand and grabbed the pistol before the Texan could move. "Now see here, sir," Devol declared, "you are a bad loser. I shall not return a cent of your money. And if you cut any more capers I'll break your nose."

Because of his reputation as "head man" on the river Devol was always being challenged to butting contests, for a hefty wager, of course. "George was a great butter," said his long-time gambling partner "Canada Bill" Jones, "He could use his head with terrible effect and kill any man living by butting him." Devol himself wrote about his remarkable skull in his autobiography *Forty Years a Gambler on the Mississippi*, published in 1887:

"I don't know just how thick my old skull is; but I do know it must be pretty thick or it would have been cracked many years ago, for I have been struck some terrible blows on my head with iron dray pins, pokers, clubs, which would have split any other man's skull wide open. Doctors have often told me that my skull was nearly an inch thick over my forehead."

When he was working the steamboat *John Walsh* out of New Orleans, Devol was challenged by the steamer's fireman, a huge brute who had won many butting contests. George placed a bet of 500 dollars on his own head and the two men squared up. "We both rushed like frenzied bulls," wrote Devol. "I gave him a glancing blow that skinned his head for about three inches. The next time there was a crash that jarred the boat and drew a shriek of terror from the passengers as the fireman fell with a thud to the deck."

Although Devol was a master at most games of chance, especially at three-card monte, he was a sucker at playing faro. In his forty years of gambling he won some two million dollars. "I will admit that I had not enough sense to keep it," he confessed in his book, "but if I had never seen a faro bank I would be a wealthy man today."

It is said that Devol's partner, Canada Bill Jones, first gave the classic gambler's answer to a friend who warned him about joining a rigged game. "Bill, don't you know this game is crooked?" To which fatalist Bill replied, "Yes, but it's the only game in town."

○

MYTHS OF THE WEST

Over the last one hundred years many myths and legends have grown around the famous characters and events of the Wild West. For example, it is widely believed that Billy the Kid was a left-handed gunslinger whose real name was William Bonney, that General Custer and the entire Seventh Cavalry were wiped out in the Battle of the Little Bighorn, and that Wyatt Earp was a true-blue peace officer who cleaned up the lawless cowtowns with his trusty Buntline Special revolver.

But these so-called "facts," and many others — well entrenched though they have become over the years — are not true.

The myth-makers have made much of Billy the Kid. He was nothing like the handsome outlaw portrayed by film stars like Robert Taylor, Paul Newman, Audie Murphy, and Kris Kristofferson. He was an ugly little chap with protruding teeth, sloping shoulders, and a slight build of some five feet six inches. Some writers like to claim that he shot dead 21 men, "one for every year of his short, sensational life." The exact number of his victims is unknown but it is believed to be much less than the legendary 21.

The fiction that he was left-handed originated from the only authenticated photograph of him that still exists. For many years the photograph was always printed in reverse, thus giving the false impression that he was left handed. Like most other notorious gunfighters, Billy was not an enthusiast of the honourable, man-to-man quick draw shoot-out, but preferred to get the better of his man by trickery or ambush.

Incidentally, another modern myth is the low-slung gun holster tied to the leg, the supposed "trade mark" of the professional gunfighter. In fact the real Westerners wore their holsters high on the hip and some noted gunmen, like Wild Bill Hickok, did not always use holsters and carried their revolvers stuck into a waistbelt, pirate fashion. And they rarely, if ever, fired their pistols two-handed in the stylized Hollywood manner; the second gun was brought into action when the first was empty or had misfired.

Frank Cahill, after he had thrown the slightly-built kid to the ground. Later, while working as a cowboy and known by the name of Bonney, he became involved in the Lincoln County War, a New Mexico range war between rival cattle outfits. Billy became an outlaw-killer with a price on his head.

Pat Garrett, a former friend of the Kid, was elected sheriff of

Left: *Billy the Kid. For many years this photograph was printed in reverse as shown here, thus giving the wrong impression that he was left handed.* Right: *Another print of the same photograph reproduced correctly.*

Most accounts of Billy the Kid give his real name as William Bonney. He did, in fact, use several names, including Henry McCarty, William Antrim, and William Bonney. Reputable Western historians now seem to agree that Billy was born in New York about 1859 and that his real name was Henry McCarty. His mother took him and his brother West and they settled in New Mexico, where his mother married a man named Antrim and Billy became known as Kid Antrim.

Popular legend tells us that he first killed at the age of twelve when he knifed a bully who had insulted his mother. In fact he slew his first victim when he was eighteen, shooting

Lincoln County in 1880 and set out to capture the young bandit. He caught him and Billy, found guilty of murder, was sentenced to be hanged. But he managed to escape from jail by killing the two deputies guarding him. Garrett went after him again, tracked him to a ranch, crept into a darkened bedroom and shot Billy dead by surprise. None of the Hollywood man-to-man nonsense here. Some years later Garrett was gunned down, shot in the back.

Custer's Last Stand is the most celebrated battle of Wild West history, in which — most people will tell you — the general was killed with the rest of his regiment. Contrary to popular belief, the Seventh

Cavalry was not totally annihilated in the fight. Custer and all those under his direct command, more than 200 troopers, were killed by swarming Indians. But the rest of the regiment, some 400 men, held out in a defensive position elsewhere on the battlefield until relieved by another column. It was nevertheless a great victory for the Indians.

general and, being the youngest to hold that rank in the U.S. Army, was dubbed the "Boy General." In 1866 he was assigned second-in-command of the Seventh Cavalry but remained the active commander of the regiment until his death.

The Battle of the Little Bighorn, 25 June 1876, was a single action in a concerted campaign involving three separ-

known is that his command, dismounted and surrounded, was overwhelmed by a great mass of warriors and all were killed. Elsewhere on the battlefield the remainder of the regiment lost nearly 100 men until rescued by the main column. Later, the Seventh Cavalry was brought up to strength and continued in service.

Wyatt Earp's reputation as a white knight of law and order is virtually wholly ficticious. And his use of the Buntline Special, a Colt sixgun with an extra-long barrel, is a complete myth. His fame as a gunfighter and prominent peace officer was largely manufactured by his biographer Stuart N. Lake, who published Earp's supposed life story in 1931. Some writers claim that Earp was a "legend in his own lifetime." The truth is that very few people indeed had ever heard of the "famous frontier marshal" before Lake's book came out.

To be fair, Wyatt Earp was no better and no worse than countless other Western drifters trying to earn a living where and how they could. Earp worked as a buffalo hunter, saloon keeper, cardsharp, sometime lawman, stagecoach guard, and was suspected of being a stagecoach robber. He was also a cool and deadly gunfighter.

Above: *George Armstrong Custer.* Top right: *A modern Butlin Special with 12 inch barrel. Contrary to popular belief, Wyatt Earp never carried such a gun.* Bottom right: *Wild Bill Hickok, photographed about 1865. Compare the way he carries his guns to that of the Hollywood gunslinger.*

George Armstrong Custer, the dashing hero of epic films and a television series was a controversial commander. His many biographers claim him to be either hero or villain; a brilliant Cavalier to some, a reckless glory hunter to others. It seems he was a paradoxical combination of both virtue and vice. A harsh disciplinarian with those under his command, he was often insubordinate and disobedient to his superiors and was once court-martialled and suspended from service for a year.

Graduating from West Point Military Academy in 1861 at the bottom of his class, Custer won fame in the Civil War as a cavalry officer. At the age of 23 he was made a brevet brigadier-

ate expeditions against the Sioux and Cheyenne. Custer's regiment, some 700 strong, was sent ahead of the main column to locate the allied Indians' encampment. Custer had orders not to attack without support. But on finding the hostile village the impetuous Custer decided to cover himself with glory by attacking immediately, confident that he and his regiment alone could defeat the Indians.

In order to attack the encampment from different directions, Custer divided his regiment. And he and his detachment galloped to their doom. His movements after separating from the rest of the regiment are shrouded in mystery. All that is definately

The Earp legend, instigated by Lake, tells us that Ned Buntline, the blood-and thunder "dime novel" writer, ordered five special .45 calibre Colt "Peacemaker" revolvers with 12-inch barrels and presented them in the summer of 1876 to the law officers he most admired, including Wyatt Earp, Bat Masterson, and Bill Tilghman. In fact there is no record of the alleged Ned Buntline order in the Colt Company's carefully maintained files, and no long-barrelled Peacemakers left the factory until December 1877. It was not a popular model and Colt produced a very small number during the frontier years. It was not until 1957 that the Colt Company, realising the legendary publicity attached to the gun, started using the official designation "Buntline Special" for its long-barrelled Peacemaker model, which is

COLT BUNTLINE SPECIAL 45

still manufactured today in various calibres.

According to Stuart N. Lake, the Buntline became Earp's favourite weapon and he often employed the long barrel as a club to knock badmen senseless. However, the other recipients of the monster revolvers found the long barrel inconvenient and cut them down to standard length. Legend further informs us that Earp's fabulous gun was lost many years ago. Thus none of the original Buntlines remain to prove the truth of Lake's story. The truth is that Earp never carried a Buntline Special. Lake created the myth and other writers have embellished it.

Wyatt Earp and his brothers Virgil and Morgan, aided by Doc Holliday, emerged the victors from the West's most celebrated shoot-out: the Gunfight at the O.K. Corral, in Tombstone, Arizona, on 26 October 1881.

For many years it has been generally understood that the fight was a showdown between lawmen and villains, with the Earp faction representing law and order. Most of the people in Tombstone at the time held another view. "To be plain," said an eyewitness, "it was simply a fight between stage robbers, and was getting rid of a lot of bad eggs on both sides. The good citizens said nothing and let it go on."

After serving as a policeman in Wichita, Kansas, and then as assistant marshal of Dodge City, Kansas, Wyatt and his brothers together with Doc Holliday moved to Tombstone, where they were known as the Earp gang. Virgil Earp became the town marshal and Wyatt worked as a shotgun messenger with a stagecoach company. Business and political rivalry between the Earps and the Clanton-McLaury gang resulted in the Gunfight at the O.K. Corral.

Intent on settling matters once and for all with the other mob, Virgil Earp took the precaution of deputising his brothers and Holliday. In other words he decided to use the shield of the law to settle a private dispute. Sheriff Behan attempted to stop the Earps as they marched purposefully towards the O.K. Corral but they brushed him aside.

The fight did not take place inside the corral as Hollywood has so often depicted, but outside the corral, on Fremont Street. Hollywood also presents the fight as a protracted shootout, in fact it was all over in less than a minute. Eyewitness accounts differ in many ways. Some said that the Earps opened fire without just cause, others claim that they shot in self defence. All that is certain is that both sides opened fire at close range and that the two McLaury brothers and Billy Clanton were shot dead. Virgil and Morgan Earp were wounded; Wyatt and Doc Holliday emerged unharmed. The latter two were arrested on murder warrants but later discharged.

Wyatt Earp lived on to the age of eighty dying virtually unknown in Los Angeles in 1929. Two years later Stuart N. Lake's controversial biography was published. Virgil Earp's widow denounced the book as "a pack of lies." Nevertheless, Hollywood and writers of fictionalised "history" seemed determined to follow the dictum "When truth and legend conflict — print the legend."

HE RUNS THROUGH THE NIGHT, AS HE HAS BEEN RUNNING FOR HOURS. ALONE. DESPERATE...

FAR FROM A HOME THAT IS NO LONGER HIS HOME, AN INDIAN DEEP IN THE WHITE MAN'S LAND...

WITH TWO IMPLACABLE PURSUERS BEHIND HIM AND DEATH AT HIS SHOULDER...

UNLESS HE CAN FIND SAFETY AND SANCTUARY AT THE 'LAZY ACE' RANCH...

WHAT THE BLUE-EYED..?

BUFFALO HEELS? THAT YOU?

DERWENT DEXTER'S DIRTY DEEDS

"YOU KNOW OLD DANCING HORSE... SOFT IN THE HEAD! SO HE SIGNED...

THANK YOU, CHIEF! YOU WON'T HAVE TO WORRY ABOUT THE LAND PROBLEM ANY MORE NOW...

BECAUSE YOU JUST SIGNED A DEED THAT MAKES EVERYTHING YOU OWN MINE!

"HE WOULDN'T GIVE THE PAPER BACK, AND WHEN SOME OF THE WARRIORS TRIED TO TAKE IT...

"HIS MEN SHOT AND WOUNDED THREE OF THEM, AND ORDERED ALL OUR PEOPLE OFF THE LAND IN FIVE DAYS...

"SO WHEN I CAME BACK AND FOUND OUT WHAT HAD HAPPENED, I DECIDED TO COME HERE LOOKING FOR HELP..."

DANCING HORSE SIGNED THE DEED WITHOUT KNOWING WHAT IT SAID? HASN'T HE GOT ANY BRAINS AT ALL?

NOT SINCE HE TOOK TO DRINKING FIRE-WATER...

DEXTER GAVE HIM THAT, TOO...

BUT THERE MUST BE SOME WAY TO STOP THIS! MY FATHER LIVED IN THESE HILLS, AND HIS FATHER, AND HIS...

YEAH, FOR MORE GENERATIONS THAN YOU'VE GOT FINGERS AND TOES TO COUNT THEM ON...

EVEN SO, THERE'S NOTHING WE CAN DO TONIGHT, BUT TOMORROW MORNING...

HMM...

LISTEN, BOYS, I THINK WE CAN SORT THIS OUT MORE FRIENDLY-LIKE! HOW ABOUT WE PLAY POKER FOR THE DEED?

POKER?

SO, AFTER A FEW MINUTES CONSULTATION...

ALRIGHT, STRANGER... POKER IT IS...

THEN HOW ABOUT WE PLAY AT THE RED OX SALOON IN SWEETWATER? TOMORROW MORNING AROUND NINE...

AND ON THE WAY BACK TO TOWN...

YOU SURE THIS IS A GOOD IDEA, BRET? AWFUL LOT DEPENDING ON A POKER GAME...

LISTEN, I CAN FEEL A LUCKY STREAK COMING ON! FOR A START, THEY OBVIOUSLY DON'T KNOW WHO I AM...

BUT NEXT DAY...

ON THE OTHER HAND, MAYBE THEY DO KNOW WHO I AM! THEY'VE BROUGHT IN FINGERS O'DIAMOND...

THE LOWEST DIRTIEST, CHEATINGEST SIDE-WINDER BETWEEN HERE AND THE PECOS..!

HOWDY, FINGERS WHEN'D THEY LET YOU OUT OF JAIL?

CAN THAT, MAVERICK! FIGURED WE'D PLAY OUT HERE IN THE STREET WHERE THERE'S NO CHANCE OF YOU CHEATING...

WE'LL CHECK OUR GUNS, TOO... MEANING THAT DERRINGER UP YOUR RIGHT SLEEVE...